Diverse and Different

Level 7 – Turquoise

Helpful Hints for Reading at Home

The graphemes (written letters) and phonemes (units of sound) used throughout this series are aligned with Letters and Sounds. This offers a consistent approach to learning, whether reading at home or in the classroom.

HERE IS A LIST OF PHONEMES FOR THIS PHASE OF LEARNING. AN EXAMPLE OF THE PRONUNCIATION CAN BE FOUND IN BRACKETS.

Phase 5			
ay (day)	ou (out)	ie (tie)	ea (eat)
oy (boy)	ir (girl)	ue (blue)	aw (saw)
wh (when)	ph (photo)	ew (new)	oe (toe)
au (Paul)	a_e (make)	e_e (these)	i_e (like)
o_e (home)	u_e (rule, cube)		

Phase 5 Alternative Pronunciations of Graphemes			
a (hat, what)	e (bed, she)	i (fin, find)	o (hot, so, other)
u (but, unit)	c (cat, cent)	g (got, giant)	ow (cow, blow)
ie (tied, field)	ea (eat, bread)	er (farmer, herb)	ch (chin, school, chef)
y (yes, by, very)	ou (out, shoulder, could, you)		

HERE ARE SOME WORDS WHICH YOUR CHILD MAY FIND TRICKY.

Phase 5 Tricky Words			
oh	their	people	Mr
Mrs	looked	called	asked
could			

TOP TIPS FOR HELPING YOUR CHILD TO READ:

- Allow children time to break down unfamiliar words into units of sound and then encourage children to string these sounds together to create the word.
- Encourage your child to point out any focus phonics when they are used.
- Read through the book more than once to grow confidence.
- Ask simple questions about the text to assess understanding.
- Encourage children to use illustrations as prompts.

This book focuses on /i/ and the alternative pronunciations of its grapheme. It is a Turquoise level 7 book band.

Can you sort these words into two groups?
One group has i as in **pig**.
One group has i as in **mind**.

picnic

wild

bring

child

kind

stick

find

mint

Are you the same as the adults at home? What about the class you are in? Is each child the same? No! We are all different.

In this class, Si is different to Tim. Tim is different to Rich. Rich is different to Ida. Ida is different to Idris. The list goes on!

The important thing to remember is that we must all be kind to people. We are all different, and that is fantastic!

People's minds all operate in different ways. If I find that I am good at one thing, you might find that you are good at a different thing.

Mike likes to go into the wild in his free time. He sees which animals he can find in the woods on trips with his mum.

Look, a spider!

Irene prefers to spend her free time reading in a silent room. It is important for Irene to have some quiet time. Loud noises can make her feel stressed.

On Fridays, Irene and Mike find a quiet room and chat. Mike tells Irene about the animals he found. Irene tells Mike what she has been reading. They are good friends.

Ivan is best pals with Eli. Eli is blind, which means his sight is different to Ivan's. Eli and Ivan spend all week thinking of quizzes.

In class on Friday, they see who wins. Eli is amazing at quizzes. He catches Ivan out all the time!

Isac volunteers to help his elders. He likes to hear Lorna's tales. She cannot do it now, but she was a pilot in the past.

Speaking to people like Lorna helps Isac to not form ideas about people based on what they look like. People can surprise you!

It is not just fine to be different, it is amazing to be different! We must all be kind and remember that we are all amazing, no matter what!

©2023 BookLife Publishing Ltd.
King's Lynn, Norfolk, PE30 4LS, UK

ISBN 978-1-80505-102-2

All rights reserved. Printed in China.
A catalogue record for this book is available from the British Library.

Diverse and Different
Written by Rod Barkman
Designed by Lucy Otter

An Introduction to BookLife Readers...

Our Readers have been specifically created in line with the London Institute of Education's approach to book banding and are phonetically decodable and ordered to support each phase of the Letters and Sounds document.

Each book has been created to provide the best possible reading and learning experience. Our aim is to share our love of books with children, providing both emerging readers and prolific page-turners with beautiful books that are guaranteed to provoke interest and learning, regardless of ability.

BOOK BAND GRADED using the Institute of Education's approach to levelling.

PHONETICALLY DECODABLE supporting each phase of Letters and Sounds.

EXERCISES AND QUESTIONS to offer reinforcement and to ascertain comprehension.

CLEAR DESIGN to inspire and provoke engagement, providing the reader with clear visual representations of each non-fiction topic.

AUTHOR INSIGHT:
ROD BARKMAN

Rod Barkman is one of BookLife Publishing's most integral members. Known to other staff as Reliant Rod, he is always trying to bring his work to a new level. Rod has written multiple books for BookLife Publishing, of which he is extremely proud. Rod is a keen traveller, voracious reader and animal lover.

This book focuses on /i/ and the alternative pronunciations of its grapheme. It is a Turquoise level 7 book band.

Image Credits Images are courtesy of Shutterstock.com. With thanks to Getty Images, Thinkstock Photo and iStockphoto. Cover – AnnGaysorn, graphixmania, Pro_Vector, Roman Samborskyi, Tasha Art. 4–5 – CREATISTA, wavebreakmedia. 6–7 – Ivan Kovbasniuk, Pranay Chandra Singh. 8–9 – Ermolaev Alexander, kdshutterman, Luc Pouliot. 10–11 – Ilike, Jure Divich. 12–13 – Aleksandar Todorovic, Freeograph, Irina Starikova3432. 14–15 – Irina Starikova3432, Veronica Louro.